Britain's Dumbest Criminals

Based on stories from police officers and county court clerks around the UK

Britain's

DUMBEST

CRIMINALS

Kim Sinclair

TAKE THAT BOOKS

First published in Great Britain in 1996 by
Take That Ltd.
P.O.Box 200
Harrogate
HG1 2YR
Fax: 01423-526035
Email: sales@takethat.co.uk
Web Site: http://www.takethat.co.uk

This edition for Books UK Ltd.
Copyright © 1999 Take That Books

Cartoons by Joe Mckeough

10 9 8 7 6 5 4 3 2 1

ISBN 1-873668-36-8

TAKE THAT BOOKS

WARNING

"Remember, dumb criminals are more prolific than you may think.

So, please sleep well tonight...

...if you can get to sleep while laughing, that is!"

**ALL THE CRIMINALS IN THIS BOOK MUST
BE ASSUMED STUPID UNTIL PROVEN
OTHERWISE IN A COURT OF LAW**

Stealing on a Shoestring

A n opportunist football hooligan in London couldn't resist the chance to cash in on his way home from a game. Sitting on the front seat of a parked car was a wallet and set of house keys. Since the door was firmly locked the ever resourceful thief turned to his trusty steel-toe-capped bovver boots.

Not supple enough to actually kick the windscreen, he took off his right boot and broke the side window with one swift blow. Although he managed to grab the wallet and keys, the car alarm detectors noticed the intrusion and set the car's horn blasting out a warning.

Stopping only to put his boot back on, the thug legged it down the street away from the police who were on match duty.

But the hapless hooligan was swiftly tackled after only 30 yards - by his own boot laces! To make matters worse, he also fell on the keys and needed five stitches in his hand at the local hospital.

Shocking Revelation

A Surrey policeman had just come on duty one morning and the officer in charge asked him to take a report of theft from an electricity meter. He strolled over to the bloke at the counter and opened his notebook:

"I understand you want to report the theft of money from an electricity meter, is that right?"

"Yes"

"How did it happen"

"Well, I got this screwdriver and broke the lock off, then I took the money"

"I think you had better come inside"...

Self Addressed

A very similar bank raid was reported in Manchester. This time, instead of a map of the getaway route, the would-be bank robber's note instructing bank staff to give him the money was written on the back of a letter. As you can guess, his name and address was still on the other side.

X Marks the Spot

Months of careful planning went into a small-time bank raid in the Welsh borders. The bank had been cased out for several weeks, so the small band of robbers knew the busy times and quiet times. They also knew the layout of the bank and the quickest route back to their hideout (well, 'hideout' is a bit of a grand name for their back-bedroom).

To make sure they could 'do the job' and be off the streets within fifteen minutes, they drew up their elaborate escape route to scale and rehearsed each step of the operation. It was such a complex route that any pursuers would be thrown off course without fail.

Everything went like clockwork. The bank opened on Friday morning and half and hour later the masked front man of the gang went in. So his voice wouldn't be recognised in the small community he held up a note saying, "Put the Money in the Bag", and waved a fake pistol for effect.

The takings were more than he'd hopped for. So much so that he had to use both hands to carry the bag as he ran out of the door smack on schedule.

Staff at the bank hit their alarm buttons and the local Bobby turned up to find the counter staff in tears, the fake pistol and a perfectly scaled map of where to find the gang. Unable to find a blank piece of paper, another member of the gang had used the reverse of their 'escape' map for the hold-up note. It was so useful that another police car was waiting outside the gang's house when they arrived back with their booty.

Mail Order Madness

Most credit card fraud is perpetrated by people whose job entails them coming in contact with card details. They then use the card number and real customer's details in different shops to obtain goods. So long as they don't attempt to purchase things above a certain level, the details won't be checked

However, one shop sales assistant in Southampton, who made a routine of keeping a personal copy of the shopper's card details, couldn't grasp the basic principles. Instead of fleecing businesses in the city, she ordered thousands of pounds worth of clothes by mail order. Although she used different names, each time she gave her home address for delivery. Very soon a special surprise arrived at the door with the postman - a fully functional policeman complete with dated search warrant.

Mellow Yellow

A prisoner was so desperate to get out of jail that he spent two days covering himself from head to toe with a yellow highlighter pen. The plan was to make the warders think he had jaundice so they'd transfer him, by ambulance, to the prison hospital. On the journey he would then jump up and escape from the vehicle.

Apparently he coloured every part of his body, including his privates, in the attempt to fool the warders. But his plan was blown apart when a warder spotted him through the inspection hatch on a midnight round colouring his face.

"The prisoner was convinced he could carry it off," said the warder, "but he was so yellow that if he'd had real jaundice he'd have probably died."

Software Solution

The soaring price of memory chips used in computers caused a spate of office thefts known as RAM raids after the name of the chips. Sometimes only the memory would be taken, but usually the thieves would simply rip the entire computer out of the office, complete with cables and attachments.

One of the East London gangs, specialised in such raids, also used to grab any boxed sets of expensive software they saw on their raids. This software would then be installed on the stolen computers to enhance the asking price when they were re-sold.

Anyone who has installed software will know that the opening screens instruct you to enter your own 'user' details, including your address. And that is just what the helpful gang did. When the police finally located some of the stolen machines, by identifying the part numbers, they only had to start up a few of the programmes to realise who was behind the raids.

Extortion Display

The introduction of digital exchanges and Caller Display by telephone companies went unnoticed by many people. One of them was a 28 year-old chancer from Norwich. He began a series of crank calls to one of his local supermarkets. Until they agreed to cough up £10,000 in used five pound notes, he said he would poison some of their products.

Unfortunately he didn't know his home phone number was being displayed every time he called.

Snatcher Bashed

An elderly Newport resident was petrified when a youth grabbed her handbag as she stood in a bus queue waiting to go shopping. However, her dismay soon turned to concern when the lad turned to run away and smacked straight into the bus-stop sign. Fellow queuers did little to stop the blood flowing from his nose as one of them applied an armlock.

Dumb Mutt 1

A Gateshead villain regularly took his dog along with him on jobs in case of trouble with rival crooks or being chased by angry householders. And so it was on a particularly inclement night in November.

By the third house on his list he was becoming fairly despondent. All the householders were at home. Desperate to get home out of the bad weather, the villain decided to take the risk and have a go at an occupied house.

So he tied his dog to the garden gate, from where he'd been observing the house, and headed up the path. But as he forced the back door he heard the sound of a police siren coming in his direction.

Fearful that he'd been spotted, he jumped into an adjoining garden and made off into the night leaving his unfortunate hound to take the can.

Can you imagine the police's delight when they arrested the mutt and found the crook's name and address on the dog's tag?

The Great Capture

Two unemployed school leavers broke into their old school looking for mischief and intent on causing some damage. After going through three classrooms they were in the gym when they heard the noise of approaching feet. Afraid of being caught, they copied the war film Great Escape and hid inside the vaulting horse.

As it happens, they had broken into the school on the night of a gymnastic team practice. The pair stayed hidden for nearly 20 minutes as the horse was used for vaulting rehearsals. In the end, the constant banging and shaking took its toll and they shouted their surrender.

Dumb Mutt 2

Another dog-loving criminal, this time from Edinburgh, had a similar habit of taking his dog along. This burglar was lucky enough to get away with his haul without being detected, but he still left his pooch behind.

Although the dog didn't carry a name tag with indicting information, it did have a keen sense of direction. The police simply let the dog off it's leash and followed it all the way home.

Underground Trip

Screaming abuse at the inspector, a respectably dressed city worker, who didn't have a valid ticket, attempted to vault over the turnstiles at Kings Cross underground station. As he did so, his trouser leg caught on one of the prongs and he sprawled across the floor. Two fare-paying passengers sat on him until the transport police arrived.

Short Sighted

A man broke into an opticians shop in Chester. Being short-sighted himself, he removed his glasses while he prised open the till. But when he came to leave, he picked up the wrong pair of specs and promptly fell down four stairs, breaking his ankle. He was arrested limping up the street and bumping into lamp-posts.

Fuel Fools

An experienced gang of ram raiders from Newcastle had perfected their technique over three years. They would steal a large 4x4 for the initial crash and accompany it with a high powered sports car for the getaway.

On this occasion the chosen target was an electrical store inside a shopping precinct. All went well with the Range Rover crashing through the outer security doors, careering down the precinct and then smashing the front of the store to pieces. The gang jumped out, all hooded so as not to be recognised by the security cameras, and started collecting their booty. With only seconds until the police could be expected, they gathered everything they could and jumped into the awaiting Mercedes.

And that's when the engine, which had been roaring throughout the raid, spluttered to a halt. After stealing the car nobody had spotted that the car was almost completely out of fuel.

The gang jumped into the 4x4 as back-up only to find their sports car was blocking the way. Nevertheless they tried to go round it. But unfortunately a design fault in the shopping precinct - in that it wasn't built for overtaking - caused the second getaway vehicle to clip a massive concrete pot-plant container and overturn.

Arm Whistle-Blow

A Birmingham builder was suing his former employers for compensation after damaging his wrist in a fall on site. The company were contesting the claim and the case had gone to court. With around £10,000 at stake the solicitors had handed their notes over to their respective barristers and battle was about to begin.

But as the council for the claimant stood up to deliver his account of how the builder's wrist was now so weak he couldn't continue to work, he came to a halt. Looking at the builder, he recognised the man who had spilt his drink in a pub the night before. Although his drink had been reimbursed, he also remembered that the cause of the spillage - the builder had just won an arm wrestling contest on an adjoining table!

Cheque First

A Leeds woman became quite proficient at stealing handbags from offices and shops during staff lunch-breaks. But her luck ran out when one of the stolen credit cards was refused. She brushed the rejection aside saying, "I must have gone over my limit" and produced a cheque book.

Unfortunately, it was one she'd stolen from the same shop only two days earlier. The shop assistant instantly recognised the forgery of her own signature and called the police.

All Shot Up

Drinkers in a Birmingham pub were settling down for a pleasant evening's drinking when there was a screech of car tyres outside. Thinking it was just another pre-pubescent lad trying to prove his manhood, hardly anyone looked up. Instead they continued with their chat about football, telly and other topics of national importance.

All that changed, however, when the door burst open to reveal a couple of masked men brandishing firearms. Dressed from top to toe in black, they cut an intimidating sight. And that was their purpose. As part of an ongoing feud between city gangs, they had come in search of a rival to 'give him a warning'.

But things didn't all go to plan when they had difficulty locating their victim in the crowded pub. Moving round the room they continuously had to order petrified drinkers to get out of their way. After a couple of minutes their patience, and cool, was beginning to crack. Still they couldn't find their target. The result was an almighty argument between the two about whose job it was to do the actual recognition.

As half the drinkers looked on aghast, and the other half made a dash for door, the two masked men stood toe-to-toe swearing at one another. Then one of them attempted to raise his gun and point it at the other. But as he did so, it went off and fired a shot through his own arm. Screaming in agony he turned and ran for the door with his colleague, but they couldn't get through the rush of drinkers clambering to get away from the shooting. By the time they eventually made it into the open, the street was full of armed police.

Long Legged

Prudhoe Museum called in the police when one of their bicycles was stolen. "I can't understand why anyone would want to steal it," exclaimed the museum's director.

Why? Because the bike in question was a Penny Farthing. The police are now looking for a crook with very long legs, possibly sporting a top hat and tails.

Instant Catch

The launch of the National Lottery and the constant publicity of many a new millionaire proved too much for a stockist of the instant win tickets. Having been shown by the lottery operators how to validate a winning ticket and give out the prize money, he hit on a way of ensuring he kept all the winning tickets for himself.

Once the shop was closed for the evening, he scratched off the "void if removed" panels from all of his stock. By entering the code number below this panel into his terminal he was informed which were winning tickets without having to touch the main ticket windows. He then kept those and processed the prizes into his own pocket.

All would have been fine if hadn't sold the losing tickets in his shop... and the customers hadn't noticed the missing panels... and the operators hadn't spotted the unusual pattern of 120 winners between the hours of 2 and 3 a.m.... and the media hadn't surrounded his shop... and he hadn't blamed his four year-old child... and...

Flaked Out

On a scale of 1 to 10 for criminal activity, stealing an ice cream cornet must rank around the 0.001 level. But crime is crime, and it rarely pays off.

David Price found that lesson out to his cost at a very young age. Desperate for an ice cream on a very hot day he stood patiently in the queue. When his turn came, he ordered the biggest 99 on the list with two flakes and three scoops of ice cream. The van attendant handed it down to him and waited for the money - which was not forthcoming.

With nothing in his pocket, young Master Price turned tail and hared across the car park toward the bushes. In hot pursuit was an elderly man who had been standing in the queue and realised what was happening. But despite the encouragement of the salesman, the youngster gave his pursuer the slip.

As the pensioner was returning to the ice cream van he heard a noise in the bushes. He turned and went to investigate, where he found David choking on one of the flakes and desperate for some air. The old man administered some first aid - and then his powers of citizen's arrest.

Badger the Burglar

A couple in Pickering couldn't believe their ears. It sounded as if someone was in their house, but they weren't making the slightest attempt to keep quiet. Surely this had to be the noisiest burglar ever. And if they were so confident to make that much din, they were probably very dangerous.

Fortunately, when they picked up the phone in their bedroom, it was still working. At least the thieves hadn't thought of cutting the communications from their countryside home.

Ten minutes later, when the local constabulary arrived, the noise was still going on. The burglars were going to be caught red-handed. And they were - or rather he was - or, even more accurately, IT was. Bursting into the main living room, expecting a scuffle, the police were amazed to find a badger very much the worse for wear. Indeed it was completely blotto.

A small amount of detective work, in the light of the morning, suggested the badger's Dutch-courage had been obtained by eating fermented fruit from the garden.

Bitten by the Bug

Another would be lottery fraudster thought he could hit the jackpot by playing last week's winning numbers, ripping the date section off the top and replacing it with one from his previous week's ticket. A strip of sticky tape joining the two sections together wasn't supposed to be spotted by the lottery operators when he went to pick up his cheque for £2,000,000.

When the cuffs went on for attempted fraud, he blamed his dog for eating the two tickets and causing the confusion.

Crane Crazy

For whatever reason, a West London man climbed into a crane cab in the middle of the night. It's not known whether he intended to cause damage with the crane jib or to see if there was anything worth stealing. But he was arrested in the morning when the site workers turned up for their shift. Apparently he'd suffered an attack of vertigo and had been lying on the floor of the 170ft crane whimpering for nearly five hours.

In the Soup

"Aarg," exclaimed the annoyed customer in an expensive Surrey restaurant, "you've spilt soup on my suit!"

"Sorry, sir, I'll clean it up," replied the startled waiter who hadn't noticed his mistake while ladling the hot liquid.

"No you won't," said the customer, "this is an Armani and it needs specialist treatment."

The waiter returned to the kitchen and explained his problem to the owner. Not wanting a lawsuit on his hands, the boss rushed out and offered to pay for the cleaning 'plus a bit of compensation'. The customer accepted the offer, but told the owner it was likely to be VERY expensive.

It was only when the customer phoned up to demand £120 that the ex-chef 'smelled a fish'. It wasn't the size of the bill which alerted him, it was the demand that it be paid in cash or 'untraceable' Eurocheques. The police were informed and a man later arrested following similar complaints from restaurants around the county.

You might think it ends there, but you'd be wrong. To compound his stupidity, when he was offered bail at £2,000, he attempted to pay with... you've guessed it... Eurocheques!

Mugging Mug

To a scumbag, like a back-street mugger, a little old lady represents easy pickings. But there was something about Mrs Costa, wandering home late at night, which would have alerted the more experienced granny-basher. Still Budge and Coffman, both from Macclesfield, certainly weren't experienced, and they were also short of a brain cell or two.

Spotting Mrs Costa hobbling along the street they decided they'd relieve her of her pension and any rings she might be wearing. After following her for nearly 15 minutes, she entered a street with very little activity and not a lot of light. It was time to pounce.

Sprinting across the street, they were more interested in keeping an eye out in case they were spotted than looking closer at Mrs Costa. If they'd bothered to look, they'd have seen she was a little larger than the average Granny.

That's because Mrs Costa was really 6′2″ binman Pete Birkman. When not collecting household refuse, one of Birkman's hobbies was the local theatre company, where he'd landed the part of 'Granny Costa' in a play written by one of the group.

After an evening's rehearsal in women's shoes Pete had developed blisters and hence a realistic hobble. He also had a bad back from work which caused him to hunch over slightly. Needless to say those injuries were minor compared to the beating that Budge and Coffman received!

Party Crasher

Looking for something 'to do' on a Saturday afternoon isn't really a problem for most people. But Dave Skelton from Gravesend found most things in life a complete chore. "There's nothing to do round 'ere, I'm bored," was his usual comment to police when questioned about petty vandalism.

So it is no surprise that he chose to gate crash a wedding party with three of his mates. Apart from not appearing on the list of guests, they stuck out like sore thumbs dressed in jeans and trainers. When the well-to-do parents of the bride asked them to leave, the trio responded with a barrage of abuse. Threats of calling the police did no good either, since Skelton realised the limits of their powers in minor matters.

Egged on by his cohorts, Skelton, trying to prove his masculinity, turned to one of the waiting staff and beckoned for them to bring him a drink, "to toast the bride's parents". The girl made no attempt to give him a drink, so he made a lunge for the tray.

As he did so, his foot caught under one of the microphone wires leading to the stage. His outreached hand completely missed the drink and, as he fell, the first thing that made any contact was his jaw on the edge of the nearest table.

Later that evening, as the party was still in full swing, Skelton was escorted from the hospital, where his jaw had been pinned, to the police station for a spot of cell crashing.

Tweedle Dumb and Tweedle Dumber

Two youths put their time in a detention centre to good use. They formed a new pairing and started turning over banks on a regular basis. One job a month and everything was OK. They always turned up on motor bikes, disguised themselves with leathers and helmets, and then split after the raid so they couldn't be followed. If one was ever caught, they had a 'blood pact' they wouldn't spill the beans on the other.

It was this standard formula which they stuck to for their raid on a high street branch in Leicester. Picking a quiet time, they marched into the lobby brandishing sawn-off shotguns and ordered everybody down onto the floor. No one disobeyed.

The first youth stood guard over the prostrate customers as the second went to the counter and demanded the money. But, in what seems to be a constant problem for bank robbers, the cashier couldn't make out what he was saying.

Aware of the time constraints he immediately took off his helmet and issued the demand again. That, of course, ensured he would be identified from the security cameras within the bank. Yet, the cashier could now tell what he was saying and the shotgun gave her motive enough to comply. And with bulging bags they roared away from the bank on their bikes in different directions.

The first youth, already identified, reached home successfully, only to be arrested one week later. The second had further to go and stopped at a petrol station on the way home.

In his first mistake, he paid for his fuel by peeling off a series of crisp new fivers from a wad which he produced from his leathers. And his second mistake was to leave his helmet behind. A suspicious worker at the station called the police, who were delighted to find the helmet owner's name and address on a sticky label inside!

Keeping Mum

An unemployed lad from York hit on a sure-fire way of providing himself with an income - he would become a bank robber. After purchasing the mandatory face mask, black clothing, and imitation firearm, he set off on his first job.

The bank he'd chosen for the first hit was one he knew well, since he held an account there. There was also the fact that his mother occasionally worked behind the counter. So he knew what security measures were in place and that a raid could be carried out with few hitches.

What he hadn't counted on was his bad handwriting. The teller couldn't read the sign he held up demanding 'all the money'. So he shouted his command, "Give me all the bloody money, and make it quick". Only to be met, from further along the counter, with, "Michael, is that you"?

His mother had been working that day and recognised his voice. Thus Michael became the only bank robber in history to drop his gun and leave the bank to the warning, "Wait till I tell your father what you've been doing".

Wrong Way

If there's a right way to rob a bank, a Lancashire pair certainly got it all wrong.

At 2 a.m. in the morning they stole a mechanical digger from a building site and drove it clanking through the streets of Rochdale towards the local branch of a high-street bank. "It sounded like a Sherman tank," said one of the residents, "it must have woken the entire population up and alerted the police for miles around."

Unaware of the attention they had already attracted to themselves the pair smashed the bucket of the digger into the wall of the bank and picked up the hole-in-the-wall cash machine. At this point a resident heard one shout to the other, "they've got us on film" as he spotted the bank's security camera.

But they were already committed and roaring the engine at an even louder level they dumped the cash machine onto the back of a waiting pick-up truck. Then they set off the wrong way down a one-way street.

Half way down the street they were met by a vehicle coming the other way. Astonished to see an oncoming car they braked hard but couldn't avoid crashing. After a brief argument with the driver of the other automobile, they stuck the pick-up in reverse and charged back up the one-way street. But if driving forward was difficult to them, going in reverse was even harder.

So as they careered toward a parked vehicle they had to brake very hard again to avoid a second collision. At this point the cash machine gave up being jostled around and slid off the back of the truck on to the floor. The pair finally realised things were going wrong and ran off into the night.

Caught in a Web

Paul Whitburn thought he'd got away with his part in an armed security van hold up in the late eighties. His part in the attack, which involved carrying one of the guns, had netted himself over £50,000. Every penny was added to his nest-egg. Another couple of successful raids, in which he acted as getaway driver, gave him enough money to 'go straight'.

More than eight years later, he'd set up a small pizza delivery business in Cornwall. His experience of house robbery gave him the ability to work late into the night and the business thrived - money was no longer a problem.

Some of his ill gotten gains had been invested in the latest computer set-up to allow him to track customers orders. It also gave him the chance to greet regulars by name and display their last few orders on screen. This proved to be another success and Paul looked for new ways of using technology for financial benefit.

It was then that a friend introduced him to The Internet, and the World Wide Web in particular. Within weeks the industrious pizza parlour purveyor had created a Web page and proudly displayed his range of pizzas for Cornish surfers to order. "Pizza by Paul" was the banner which greeted visitors to his page, and then a picture of the proud owner appeared before the strap-line "come in and look at my delicious pizzas..."

Perhaps it was bad luck, perhaps he thought it was too long ago, and perhaps he underestimated the number of Internet users, but within two weeks his picture had been recognised and the police alerted.

Shift Work

One of the major tasks for a house robber is to observe any possible targets and get an idea of the comings and goings of the residents. Most robbers don't like to enter an occupied house, and if they do they like the occupants to be well asleep. That means many hours have to be spent late into the night.

One hapless thief found the late nights too much to handle. He was in the middle of passing through the house, looking for anything worth taking, when he was disturbed by noises from the next door bedroom. Although one of the beds in the room was occupied by the family's teenage son, he jumped into the other to avoid detection if anyone came in.

The problem is he fell asleep and was still there in the morning when the boy awoke. His next night was spent in a comfortable cell.

Marathon Mistake

Tyler Brown made his living picking the pockets of rich foreigners visiting the capital. Over the years, he'd perfected his technique so that virtually nobody could detect his handiwork. But even if they did so, he had an ace up his sleeve - or rather his trousers. For Tyler was an above average athletics club runner, specialising in the 100m and 200m sprints. Thus, if anyone discovered his activities and tried to 'have a go' he could be sure of a swift getaway.

However, he bit off more than he could chew when he tried the pockets of Yatsua Mutsoko. The little Japanese man was barged by Tyler while he was queuing to get into the Tower of London. And as the pickpocket went past, Yatsua felt Tyler's hand reach inside his breast pocket and grab his wallet. Despite his almost complete lack of knowledge of the English language, he managed to shout out "stop". But like residents of large cities around the world, no-one around tried to intervene or block Tyler's path.

Not about to give up his hard earned Yen for anyone, Yatsua gave chase. Predictably Tyler out-sprinted his pursuer and turned a street corner. But his relief turned to dismay when the familiar sound of a "stop" in a Japanese accent echoed down the street. Tyler set off again and put more distance this time between himself and the little man. Yet once again, when Tyler slowed down the word "stop" reached his ears.

Four more times the Londoner sprinted away, but before long his stamina began to wane and the little Japanese man closed the distance. Dismay turned to desperation for Brown as the race went on and Yatsua closed ever nearer on his prey. In the end, he just couldn't summon the energy to run away any longer and he held the wallet out.

Yatsua Mutsoko, or Sensei Mutsoko as he is known to his karate pupils, reached out further than the wallet and put Tyler in a painful arm-lock until someone called the police. It was only when a translator turned up to take statements at the police station, that Tyler discovered Yatsua was not only a black-belt at karate, but a sub 2hr 30 minute marathon runner.

Immature Whisky

Agent walked into an off-licence in Greater Manchester and started looking round the store. Taking furtive glances all around him and not concentrating on any products, he immediately stood out to the security cameras. Thus it was no surprise when he eventually landed upon the whisky rack and helped himself to a bottle. Of course, this didn't go in his shopping basket, it went under his raincoat and out of sight.

The security cameras continued to follow him around the store until he passed through an empty checkout and made for the door. At that point one of the plain clothed store detectives stepped forward. Aware that the game was up, the man dropped his whisky, pushed the detective out of the way and legged it into the crowd of shoppers as fast as he could.

But in all the commotion he left behind one important item - his four year-old son, who'd been taken along to make it look like a normal shopping expedition.

Falling into Trouble

Reading doesn't always figure high on a crim's list of activities. So it is not entirely surprising that Mike and Warren Booker failed to notice the warning signs when they broke into a city centre house. All they had spotted was that the owners were obviously out and the door wasn't locked.

As they walked through the house, it became evident that the owners hadn't been around for a long time and all their possessions had been taken out, apart from the carpets. "They've probably moved house and nobody's moved in here yet," suggested Warren.

"Yeah, there's nothing worth taking here," replied Mike, "let's move on."

"No," continued Warren, "look again."

"Where"

"Along the walls," said Warren enigmatically, "the plumbing's still here, and our builder mate Kevin will pay us good money for these radiators and pipes."

"Good idea," said Mike catching on quick, "How do we get it out?"

"We can get our tools and be back here within 15 minutes, it's a cinch."

Sure enough, Mike and Warren headed out into the night and returned with a borrowed bag full of wrenches, spanners and crow-bars. Before long the first radiators were out and the haul was growing. In fact it was growing too easily, the walls hardly seemed to offer any resistance when hit with the bar - they just crumbled. Being thieves, they weren't too bothered how the goods came out, so long as it was quickly.

Half way through the job, Mike stopped. "What's that noise," he said, thinking they'd been rumbled. "Oh, it's probably just part of the system emptying," replied Warren. But he was VERY wrong. Because the house they were ripping apart had already been condemned as extremely dangerous and on the point of collapse.

The first the pair knew of this was when one of the doors fell in, followed by copious amounts of brickwork. Then they noticed the wall they were working on was starting to disintegrate. Faced with being buried under a ton of rubble, the pair chose the safer option and fled the scene.

In the morning the house was almost totally demolished, and most people thought it had fallen down of its own accord. But unfortunately for the brother, the fire brigade had to be called because a neighbour reckoned he could smell gas. As they sifted through the rubble looking for the leak, they came across the bag of tools complete with Kevin's wallet containing his address.

Take Two

B ank raiders on the Isle of Wight realised their every move was being recorded on the camera positioned in the corner of the room. But they continued with their raid nevertheless, masked only by tights over their heads.

Three bags of cash and notes were filled and the gang made ready to run. Then came the master stroke of their plan. One of the gang pulled a chair out of one of the interview booths, dragged it to the corner, and ripped down the camera. They could now escape safe in the thought that they wouldn't be recognised.

Unfortunately for the gang, the whole raid was being recorded at a remote site. And the otherwise difficult task of enhancing the pictures, to get a clear image, was removed thanks to an excellent close-up of the guy who stole the camera.

Garden Grabbers

With people prepared to pay ever bigger prices, theft of garden plants is on the increase. In some cases whole gardens, including the lawn, have been taken while the owners were away. But not all the thieves are working in familiar territory.

Wayne Bright, from Reading, fell into the latter category. More used to stealing video recorders and televisions, he wasn't at home in his own garden, let alone someone else's. So like most villains, he resorted to the concept that the bigger the plant, the more it was worth.

While such an equation can be applied to several species, it most certainly doesn't include ornamental hogweed. Unaware of the consequences, he dug up two towering specimens from a garden in the east of the town.

Both were in full bloom and had reached well over six feet in height. They had taken some digging up, saving the roots, but they were obviously 'big'.

Two hours later he was feeling distinctly itchy. After three hours he was in pain. And after four hours his sores were starting to weep. Five hours and he was in the casualty department and six hours he was answering police questions.

If he had only waited until nightime, he could have saved himself a lot of discomfort, since hogweed usually only causes irritation if you come in contact with it in bright sunlight.

Gormless Golfer

A customs official beckoned over a visiting German golfer as a routine check at Dover ferry port. The man was well dressed and explained he was looking forward to a spot of golf between business meetings he'd arranged in Kent.

Being a keen golfer himself, the official enquired into the German's handicap. But he was perplexed by the answer, "I don't have a handicap, I'm very fit at present".

So he tried another question - "How many birdies are you hoping to shoot?"
"None," replied the tourist, "I don't believe in blood sports and shooting birds is illegal in Germany".

Smelling a rat, the customs man asked the German to demonstrate his swing. This he executed perfectly, but in reverse.

A significant amount of narcotics were found in his bag!

Bad Case

Some robbers just don't prepare for their job properly. One erstwhile bank robber fell decisively into this category. Spotting a street-level window into the basement of a bank, he decided to 'have a go' and see what he could find.

Whether he thought he would find piles of bank notes sitting around on tables isn't clear. Still he smashed his way through the toughened glass and squeezed himself through the gap. But as he did so, he cut himself quite badly. Once inside, dismayed already at the sight of his own blood, he started to panic when he realised he wouldn't be able to get back out of the window without causing himself even more damage. And, surprise, surprise, the cash he'd hoped to steal was hidden away in the safe.

There was little option but to pick up the phone and call 999. Realising the game was probably up, but ever the optimist, he asked for the ambulance and then, when they arrived, tried to persuade them he'd already informed the police.

All Change

Unlike most of the offenders in this book, this one got clean away with his crime. He walked into a 7-11 shop in London and waited until he was the only customer in the shop. When he was sure he was alone, he walked up to the cashier and placed a £20 note on the table and asked if the cashier could change it for him.

But as the helpful employee opened the till, the man produced a pistol and waived it in her face. "Give me all the money," he demanded menacingly.

Convinced he meant it, and more concerned for her life than her employer's takings, the clerk did as she was told. The crook grabbed the money, put his gun away and fled leaving the £20 note on the table.

The total amount in the till - £15.36

Open and Shut Case

An opportunist thief in Liverpool spotted a car with its side window partially down. Not able to resist the temptation, he reached inside and pressed the small electric window button to open the window more fully. However, he pressed it in the wrong direction and the window closed on his arm.

This wouldn't have been so bad, but it closed on an artery and cut off the supply of blood. As a result he couldn't move his fingers properly and press the other end of the control, and the gap was now too small for the other arm to reach through.

He was still there when the owner returned.

Horse Torque

A specialist team of horse thieves had been known to be operating in the Newmarket area. But one night they got everything wrong.

The team of three turned up as usual with their horse box towed by a Volvo. It should have been the night before, but they'd decided to wait another day because of very heavy rain and thunder the previous night. With such inclement weather, they thought there was a high risk of a stable hand being around to comfort the horses. However, the rain had stopped a couple of hours beforehand, enabling them to get on with the job of stealing a prized stud stallion.

The first two horse thieves broke their way into the stables and calmed the horse. Then they tied specially made cloth shoes to its feet and led it into the yard. The other member had lowered the horse box door and helped them lead it up the ramp. It was only then, by the light of a lamp in the box, that they spotted they'd got the wrong horse.

A bit worried about their mistake, they took the first horse back to the stable and returned with another. Still this wasn't the one they wanted. So on their third trip all three went to select the right horse. This time they got it right and led their stead into the box. The whole operation had taken over twenty minutes and everyone wanted to get away quickly.

But as they tried to pull away, they realised the car wheels were skidding on the gravel. One of the tyres was in a very small ditch on the corner of the entrance to the stables. Not being a four-wheel-drive, the more they accelerated the Volvo, the more the free wheel span.

Very soon, due to the sodden conditions, it had developed a small ditch of its own and the rear axle of the car was touching the gravel. The team made a vain attempt to lift the car out with the help of a spade, having detached the horse box, but to no avail. And they fled the scene, leaving their car, the horse box and their shovel.

On a Plate

Families with more than one car often park the most expensive in the garage, lock the door, and then park the 'second' car in front. The idea being that thieves wouldn't be interested in the cheap car, and not bother breaking into the garage.

Yet an amazing amount of cars parked in this configuration still get stolen. The reason is the immense amount of profit that can be made from expensive cars such as Mercedes and Lotuses, and the efficient networks they establish to whisk the cars out of the country within a few hours of being stolen.

One such robbery didn't run with such efficiency though. The thieves had targeted a brand new Ferrari parked in the garage of a country house in Buckinghamshire. In front of the garage was a 'K' reg Fiesta, which they would have to move first.

On a windy night, ideal for covering any noise they would make, the car thieves arrived with their pick-up truck and an adapted removals lorry. The pick-up would be used to move the Fiesta, then the Ferrari would be towed or driven into the back of the removals truck and driven off to the motorway only three miles away.

Although they were used to 'trading' with brand new cars, they hadn't invested in one themselves. And the pick-up truck wasn't exactly the latest model. After hitching the rope to the front of the Fiesta, it didn't come as any surprise to find that the pick-up didn't start first time. Indeed it took four goes to get the engine turning over again. Then, as they took up the strain, they realised that dragging the other car along the gravel may be more difficult than the normal driveway tarmac because the pick-up's wheels were spinning.

For almost five minutes they continued trying to drag the small car out of the way to get at their prize. But as time went by tempers began to fray, and their chances of being detected increased. So one of the members decided it was time to throw a bit of caution to the wind, and rev the pick-up a little higher. There may be more noise, but it would give them more power and, anyway, the storm would mask the noise. And this he did, putting his foot on the accelerator pedal, he gave the three litre engine more juice and the pick-up moved forward.

Unfortunately for the gang, the reason for the sudden movement was that the rear bumper had come away from the pick-up. Also, the noise of the breakage was loud enough to wake the inhabitants who promptly switched on their security lights. Realising the game was up, the gang departed at high speed, leaving behind their bumper complete with identifying number plate.

Puss in Boots

A Glaswegian cat-burglar managed to effect entry, through a skylight, into a small plate-glass company's head office. Once inside he went straight over to the brand new safe and opened it using numbers he'd picked up by sifting through rubbish discarded over the previous week from the office.

Delighted at the haul of nearly £1,000 he danced around the deserted office in pleasure. However, his joy was short lived and his expression turned to pain when he crashed straight through a two-metre square piece of plate glass which had been put in the office for a staff demonstration the following morning. Luckily he didn't sever any arteries. But there was still enough blood to make him panic and phone for an ambulance. Not one, but two blue flashing lights were on the scene within 10 minutes.

Pushed to the Limit

Yet another bank robber marched up to the cash desk and produced a gun together with the standard note saying to "hand over all the money" (This method seems so common that someone could probably start a business making the signs).

But this guy got a totally unexpected response. Instead of complying with his wishes, or trying to stall him, a solid steal shutter shot up between him and the bank clerks. The whole thing was extremely quick, and for a couple of seconds the raider looked blankly at the security screen. Then the situation dawned on him - he was about to be caught. So he ran to the door and tried to push it open. It didn't move!

Obviously this was part of the super security measures at the bank. He was trapped. In a desperate attempt to free himself he first smashed at the door with his elbow. Then he tried kicking it in. But the reinforced glass held firm. Then he raised the barrel of his gun and smashed away at the glass. Still it refused to break. If the gun had been real, he'd have probably tried blasting the lock, but it had been disabled by the original owner.

Completely frustrated he ran at the security screen and banged on it yelling warnings of what he'd do if they didn't open the door. Needless to say, the staff didn't even bother to respond. Finally, and this was all captured on the bank's security cameras, he fell to his knees crying at his bad luck and the abilities of modern security devices.

It was only when the police arrived and pushed open the door from their side, that he realised all he had to do was PULL the door handle.

The Garage Robber

Similar screen protection devices operate in a few petrol stations, where cashiers are often subjected to attack/robbery/lonely pensioners dropping in for a chat.

Captured on the site's security cameras, film shows a wiry, woolly hatted man attempting to rob the till by simply ordering the female cashier to hand over the loot.

When she doesn't, he reaches over the counter, where the screen is clearly signposted and on view, and presses the 'Open' button of the till. He then proceeds to jump on the counter, kneel down and grab handfuls of cash from the register.

As the robber is engrossed in his sixty second snatch routine, the cashier presses another button which shoots the screen up, right into the robber's stomach, and lifts him into the air to pin him against the ceiling. Unfortunately he managed to wriggle free, fall down, and get away, though he was traced and locked up through the video evidence.

You're Welcome

Thieves broke into a warehouse in Northampton and stole two pallets containing boxes of small, seaside gift trinkets. The stock had been placed in storage by the manufacturing company almost a year earlier.

"I don't know what they are going to do with them," said the marketing manager for the manufacturers, "we had fifteen sales reps on the road for six months and we couldn't sell any of them."

He continued, "They were one of our worst commercial mistakes and we found we couldn't even give them away. In a way, you could say this robbery was helpful. I'd been wondering what to do with them, and up until now we've been paying for the storage."

Lick That

The ever increasing cost of stamps hits everyone where it hurts most - in the pocket.

But James Gibson, from Middlesbrough, thought of a way round the problem. Running a small, mail-order, pornography business, his profits were taking a severe beating. So he resorted to printing his own stamps. Having sourced a suitable weight and quality of paper, and the correct ink, he set to work.

Printing the sheets of stamps was the easy bit. But putting the perforations into the sheets, in a way which wouldn't be spotted immediately, was a much more difficult task. Hour after hour, night after night, he spent with a small pointer, putting rows of little holes into the sheets.

The result was very impressive and to the eye nobody could tell the difference. Once they were on an envelope, it was even harder to spot the forgery. But the post-office doesn't rely on 'the eye' for franking and sorting its mail. Each authentic stamp has a series of virtually invisible phosphorous bands on the surface. So, Mr Gibson's painstakingly created forgeries showed up as soon as he started to use them.

Stamp forgeries are quite common, but finding the source of the fakes is usually a different matter. Most forgers sell their handiwork and the end users aren't usually aware of the scam. Indeed, they may have bought them from a local retailer, who has also obtained them through normal routes.

But James Gibson was arrested within two days - because he'd put his return address on the back of each envelope he'd posted!

Press Complaint

Many small pressure groups find the only way to draw attention to themselves is to resort to violence of some sort. And that is the route which a three-strong band of animal rights activists from Wales chose to tread. Most of their activities centred around breaking into laboratories where animals were rumoured to be used in experiments. Once inside they would cause damage to equipment and release any animals they came across.

On one of their break-ins, these activists came across a home address list of the senior researchers at the labs. Believing these people to be the pinnacle of their hatred, they decided to send each one an incendiary bomb, with the aim of seriously burning their victim.

Not having experience of bomb making in the past, the leader set upon an information gathering exercise. By scouring old wartime books, reference libraries, and the Internet, he was able to gather the information he needed and build a functional, if rudimentary, parcel bomb. Proud of his handiwork, he sent the first 'sample' out to the researcher at the top of his list.

That evening he listened in to the local radio to learn the fate of his victim. But to his horror, he heard only of a letter bomb which had failed to go off. Intent on finding out what he'd done wrong, he called the police and found out that a press conference was scheduled for the following morning.

Next day, dressed as smartly as he could muster, he went to the nearby station and posed as a freelance reporter. The usual questions were asked; who would do such a thing?; what would be their motivation?; and did they have any suspects? But still he was no closer to finding out what went wrong. So he summoned the courage and started asking questions about the device. Slowly he found out what they knew and why they thought it had failed to ignite when opened.

"But that can't be right," he blurted, "I definitely connected the blue wire to the positive terminal."

Celebrating in Style

Since the advent of the common market, customs officials have had a difficult time controlling the amount of alcoholic drink being brought into the country. The rules say is an individual is allowed to bring in as much beer as they like so long as it is for personal consumption.

Many people, however, travel over to the continent purely to stock up on large amounts of duty free beer and champagne. When they return, they sell their smuggled liquor to unscrupulous publicans or on the street at a vast profit.

Malcolm Hedge was one of those seeking to make a quick profit. All week he'd been travelling over to France on a variety of ferries. Each time he came back with a different van full to the brim with cans of strong lager. For the first four days his luck was in and he was waved through customs. But on the fifth day he was pulled over for a 'random check'.

Amazed at the amount of alcohol he was transporting Mal pulled out a story about getting it for his daughter's wedding. This, according to the rules, was perfectly acceptable, and Mal could tell things were going his way. So to seal the proceedings he waded in with lots of bon-homie and good natured chat.

It worked a treat and everyone around started to relax. Mal told them how he'd initially disliked his future son-in-law but come round to the idea. He also described how it was going to be the best day of his life and the lager would see to that.

"You should come along," he said in jest to one of the customs officers, "you're working too hard. I've seen you on duty every day this week."

In the Bag

This one was reported by several policemen around the country. All swear blind that THEIR stories are completely true. However, the coincidences are so great, it is most likely an Urban myth. Nevertheless...

A robber marched into a post-office and stood in line. When he reached the front, he produced a gun, announced it was a stick-up and pulled a hefty paper bag over his head. Unfortunately he'd forgotten to cut any eye holes in it.

Motorbike Madness

A Harley Davidson motorbike is a treasured possession of all owners. As any owner will know, these bikes are big and heavy, and need a certain amount of strength to be moved.

Also, the lengths owners will go to in order to protect their machines are legendary. These include keeping them in the house instead of the garage to deter erstwhile burglars.

You can imagine the joy that eight stone James Tracker felt when he broke in to a Streatham semi one morning whilst the occupants were at work. There in front of him in the kitchen, resting by the unused fireplace was a gleaming vintage Harley Davidson motorbike, with the keys in the ignition. Surely only dreams were made of this.

Tracker jumped on the machine and play-revved the throttle as he tried to figure out who he could sell the machine to, and for how much. Re-enacting a movie scene he jumped hard on the gas pedal expecting the animal beneath him to rumble into orgasmic life. Instead there was silence and he felt himself moving ever so slowly through air.

The next thing he saw was the light of an Emergency rescue crew in his eyes. He was looking up into the faces of strangers in blue uniforms. As you may have guessed, the bike had toppled over taking the would be, but very slight, thief with it as they crashed on to the old tiled floor. Tracker was knocked out cold and was found by the owner's early lunchtime return. He was charged with aggravated exit.

Strange Sensation

Car crime is a major worry to owners, the police and insurance companies. Every year another 'sure fire protection system' for cars is announced, only to be foiled by the ever clever thief and stupid owner. Hot hatches have proved irresistible for teenage car thieves.

However, one Silverstone-dreaming teenager, Craig Evans, from Wigan, rues the day he stole a white Astra GTi from outside a Post Office. Seeing the car parked at the road side, driver's window open, keys in the ignition, temptation got the better of him. Casually he opened the door, sat down and drove off. The car's owner, Mr J. Carmichael was unaware of the event as he waited in the queue at his Post Office to pay his gas bill.

Half a mile down the road Evans saw two school friends. Pulling over he asked them to get in if they wanted a fun ride on the dual carriageway.

Travelling safely at 60mph Craig started to giggle and asked his fellow passengers to stop messing about. They denied it, but he insisted that if they didn't stop tickling his ankle he would crash.

It was just then that a Police patrol car noticed the white Astra in front do a massive right then left swerve before pulling up on the left verge, tyres leaving a trail of acrid smoke. Stopping some two hundred yards ahead the officers jumped out to see two teenagers running away and one frantically trying to get his trousers off.

There's a "****ing snake up my leg" was the response the officer was given when he asked what was up. Having assisted in the removal of the trousers, with no sight of the snake, the officers checked the car.

Coiled up under the driver's seat was a small grass snake. Mr Carmichael has no idea how the snake came to be in his car, but he recommends it as a deterrent to joy riders. He now locks his car wherever he goes.

Four x Four x Far

The adverts for the increasingly popular 4x4 cars show them climbing Everest, wading through white water rapids and attempting other feats which mere normal cars could not even contemplate. Needing no additional driving skill means they have proliferated on the roads, and in the 'missing property, presumed stolen' list at the police station.

Many 4x4 owners want the rugged look of a 4x4 but the sophistication of a rear window wiper, central locking, and electric windows. It is to these sophisticated extras that Joshua Smilie owes his thanks and the safe return of his new £33,000 Range Rover.

The car was stolen from the Henley Show by two young farm apprentices. Fed up with having to drive tractors and old tin can Suzuki's, the lads, worse the wear for a trip to the show's beer tent, found some spare car keys on the bar.

As their luck would have it, trying a few of the doors of the 4x4's parked nearby, they matched key to door. Sober they might have stopped at this point, but bravado, the beer and the heat of the moment drove them to steal the car and take it off to some off-road tracks they knew nearby.

The adverts may not show it, but Range Rovers can topple over when driven at fast speed up vertical banks. This one did and fortunately the central locking system jammed as the car fell on its side. As the farm lads found out, you cannot break the windows from the inside.

So they lay trapped and sick for nearly 24 hours. Their absence was reported by worried parents, as was the car's loss by Mr Smilie. The boys, and car, were found the next day by a local farmer enjoying himself off-roading his own vehicle.

Smash and Grab

An unfortunate opportunist thief noticed a tempting wallet sitting on the back seat of a car as he walked past. Trying not to draw attention to himself, he walked back past the car for a second look. Sure enough, it was bulging with bank notes and there was the possibility of a few credit cards to boot.

On the third pass there was no-one within fifty metres, so he picked up a large stone from a nearby garden and smashed the rear window of the car. Glass went everywhere, but there was a big enough hole to reach through. Not wasting time, he put his right arm in and grabbed the wallet. And that's when Churchill grabbed his arm. The three year-old bulldog had been sleeping on the back seat just out of sight under the window.

Stupid Shopper

Have you ever found yourself pushing the wrong trolley around the supermarket. It can be very embarrassing as, carrots in hand, you search around vainly for your own trolley. Did you take theirs, or did they take yours?

Of course, if you are a shoplifter and inside your trolley is your bag with lifted goods, it can be even more important to find 'your' missing trolley. Someone who was not quite concerned might just start their shopping again, or look through the trolley in their possession and take out items they did not want. The shoplifter on the other hand, will be a bit more frantic.

It was this erratic behaviour that caught the eye of a supermarket store detective in Harrow. Used to seeing eccentric behaviour, this particular young womans' actions struck him as odd.

Why was she looking in to everyone's trolley, whilst still holding a bag of carrots. Suddenly the woman under surveillance rushed towards the checkout and swooped a bag from out of a nearly empty trolley. "I believe this is mine" she said as she walked off with it.

The elderly gentleman at the checkout seemed non-plussed and cheerfully paid for his goods and left. Not put off the security guard watched the young woman put the bag in a new trolley and finish her shopping. As she was about to leave the shop she was accosted and her bag was found to contain three bottles of whisky, not paid for.

Know How To Use It

If you have a gun you should know how to use it. This was the near fatal mistake made by J.J. Hughes when he broke in to the isolated home of a Scottish Highland family. Having heard that there were some extremely valuable stuffed animals in the home, Hughes arrived late one night.

Expecting no-one to be home he had still taken with him a shotgun stolen on a previous raid some years before. Finding a side window open, Hughes climbed in and made his way along a corridor to the library where he believed his quarry was on display.

On opening the door ahead he saw the most perfect specimens of pheasant, otter and stoat, as his information had told him. Removing the items from their displays he put them in a sack and made his way back. Ignoring the open window he walked through the kitchen and stopped dead in his tracks.

There in front of him was a huge man with a deer strung over his shoulders. Blood dripped slowly onto the stone kitchen floor. Hughes quickly raised his shotgun and ludicrously shouted 'freeze, or I'll shoot'. A Scottish brogue laughed deep and huskily as its owner raised his shotgun to match, "And so will I" it replied.

Seeing the blood dripping Hughes dropped his sack and gun and ran back to the open window. But a massive noise, fit to burst his ear drums, was followed by the window shattering in front of him.

"Don't shoot," he whimpered as he put his hands on his head. The house's owner kept watch as the rest of his shooting party arrived at the house and called the police. Hughes' empty shotgun lay pathetically abandoned on the floor.

My Name In Print

It is said that everyone would like to see their name in print. This wish resulted in a seventeen year old teenager from Stirling being jailed for three months. He had been decorating a house as part of some Community Service work he was required to do from an earlier offence. Having completed his work he stole £230 and then painted his name on the wall. Police had little trouble tracking him down and arresting him.

Man's Best Friend

" **A** dog is for life, not just Christmas," could have been the judges remarks as he passed sentence on Chris Tempest after he was charged, and found guilty, of stealing a store's charity box.

You may have noticed, even contributed, to charity boxes on the counters of stores, banks and building societies. So had Mr Tempest. One hot summers' day he and his best friend Basher (a cross between various breeds) were wandering along the high street with nothing much to do. Tempest had noticed a new 'Save The Children' fund box at his local building society the day before. Feeling peckish and with no money left he decided to steal it.

Upon entering the branch he told Basher to sit by the table and chairs, whilst he went to join the short queue. As he approached the counter where the collection box was he noticed a shopper put a £10 note in. As luck would have it this became the next free counter for him. Bluffing he asked the assistant for a leaflet and whilst her back was turned he put the box under the jacket hung discreetly over his left arm.

Without waiting for the leaflet he left quickly through the door and was away down the high street. Basher meanwhile slept soundly under the table in the nice cool building society branch. Our uncharitable friend, went off, had a meal and then realised basher was not with him. Retracing his movements he worked out that Basher must still be in the building society and he raced back there. Peering through the window he spotted his trusty friend still asleep under the table.

Tempest opened the door and whistled to his friend. But before he could do anything else he was bundled into the branch by two large uniformed police. His less than charitable actions had been caught on the security camera and the police had been called. They had banked on the fact that even a criminal would return for his dog, no matter who he chose to steal from.

Licking Good Story

Modern technology is helping to catch those in society who would rather steal than earn their living. Blackmailing, however, is a more sinister crime again. One such blackmailer threatened to poison the food at his local cash & carry unless he was given a £10,000 cash sum. Obviously the store did not want this to happen and were very worried at how it would affect their sales and their presence in the community.

The police were keen to catch the person as they knew from past experience the fear that such a threat, once known, could strike in the hearts of people. A form of mass hysteria can result whereby people believe they have been poisoned by the blackmailer when in fact it is just routine food poisoning, probably through careless food preparation.

In this case though, the blackmailer had not counted on the ingenuity of the police. He should have sent his demand letter in a pre-paid envelope, but instead he used a first class stamp and licked it himself. Saliva tests from the stamp were able to provide a DNA analysis. All the police needed now was to catch the blackmailer and match his, or her, DNA with that taken from the stamp. So the supermarket in Wolverhampton was instructed to meet the blackmailers' demand and go ahead with the release of the money.

Store staff were briefed on the event and the blackmailer was arrested as he turned up, at the store, to collect his cash as arranged. When arrested by police he insisted that he knew nothing about the blackmail and was merely picking up the suit case as part of a treasure hunt. DNA tests proved otherwise.

All Aboard

Catching criminals is all about thinking like they do and being one step ahead. A constant source of frustration to the police is the fact that they arrest someone, who gets let out on bail, and then fails to turn up at court. Believe it or not there are thousands of such cases every year. So, how do the police catch these criminals again, and keep them at a detention centre, this time for the alleged crime and failure to turn up at court? They devise a scam!

Letters were sent out inviting a 'select group of individuals' to an evening's wining and dining at a local pub. The letter stated that attendees would be able to help themselves to drinks and food all night provided they arrived promptly, brought along proof of identity, and sat through a 30 minute presentation on holiday accommodation in Spain.

As guests arrived on the damp Monday evening they were greeted by charming hostesses bearing introductory drinks and canapés. The door to the sumptuous buffet was left temptingly ajar. At 7.30 the guests were requested to make their way through to a side room with a small cine screen. At this juncture the doors were closed and warrants for the arrest of most of the male 'guests' were read out by the local police force. The criminals were led away to waiting police vans and the food was given away in the pub afterwards.

Who says there is no such thing as a free lunch?

Every Thing But The Baby

A Spanish tourist, on holiday in Dublin, had been looking at Christ Church Cathedral in the City Centre when two locals started chatting to her. Knowing Dublin to be a friendly place she relaxed and chatted with the couple. Their baby daughter slept on in her buggy unaware of her fate. Suddenly the tourist's handbag was snatched from her shoulder and the local couple ran off through the streets.

Bemused, the tourist looked at the baby in the pram. She had assumed it was the not-so-friendly couple's, but maybe not. After a few minutes when nobody came to claim the baby the woman went in to a shop and called the police.

Some hours later the baby's mother gave herself up at a local police station asking for her daughter. She was charged and then released on bail. The police were heartened by the fact that the mother thought her daughter was worth more than the handbag and its contents.

Lord of the Jungle

Police were keen to arrest a 22 year old man who they suspected of involvement in at least two armed robberies. Nottingham police were concerned that the man, who they knew to be armed, could be very dangerous and possibly engage in a violent arrest situation.

A tip off informed them that the suspect was working part time as a strip-o-gram. His act was 'Tarzan - Lord of the Jungle' which, as you no doubt realise, means that he has to prance around in a loin cloth with little more protection than a plastic banana!

Realising that he would be unable to hide a sawn-off shotgun on his person, the police hit upon the idea of booking his act for a hoax party. A female officer placed the order and was waiting for him at the party.

As is the case for such acts, she paid him cash before he 'performed'. But when the suspect went to the toilets to change he was cautioned and arrested. Apparently his expression, when being read his rights, was well worth the performance fee.

Male or Female

Police in King's Cross, London, are used to receiving calls related to muggings and bodily attacks. So when they arrived on the scene in a notorious red light street they were not unduly surprised to find a man in a suit very much the worse for wear. The man said he had been accosted by a prostitute and then beaten up. She had stolen his wallet and run off.

The police took a description of the woman and arrested a suspect later that night. The victim had described his assailant as a six foot blond wearing a tight red dress. When questioned the prostitute admitted the crime saying she had performed the services as requested and then the man had slapped her in the face and walked off refusing to pay. She had retaliated and taken his wallet.

When asked where she had learned such effective self defence, the prostitute smirked and admitted that 'she' was in fact 'a he' and in a fight could hold her own.

Red as a Lobster

Security at hospitals is a very difficult situation. There are always staff and the public coming and going at all hours of the day. Items in hospitals are very attractive to thieves, from drugs through to equipment - all can be sold for large amounts of money here and abroad.

With this in mind one thief walked into a Salisbury hospital and put on a white coat. This served to put him above suspicion so that he was able to steal pagers and other equipment. As he was about to leave the hospital he saw a modern vertical sunbed in an unoccupied room and let himself in. Stripping off he set the timer for a 45-minute session and relaxed dreaming of his newly tanned torso.

Unbeknownst to him the machine was not a normal sunbed but a medical treatment unit (unsurprising in a hospital). Used to treat skin conditions the machine should only be used for 10 seconds. As the thief's skin began to erupt into blisters he knew something was wrong.

Grabbing his clothes he made a speedy escape. By now he was in some pain and as this worsened he drove some 20 miles to the casualty department of another hospital. Staff were concerned for his health and he was admitted to their burns unit. The police were contacted by staff who were suspicious of the doctor's coat and haul of equipment.

Caught Red Eyed

Irene Wilson returned home to discover her flat in Leominster totally ransacked. While she had been out enjoying herself at a local wine bar, someone else had been enjoying sifting through her possessions. Nothing of any great value had been taken, just the usual video recorder, a couple of videos, some inexpensive jewellery and a leather jacket.

Naturally she called the police who took all the details. But as is the case with most burglaries of small items, the local bobbies told her the chance of anyone being caught were virtually nil.

Two months later she received her usual itemised phone bill with a mysterious entry. On the day of the burglary there were five phone calls, four of which she could identify the number. But the last call, made during the evening when she was out was to an unknown number. She called the police once more.

Within two days they'd made an arrest and came round to explain what had happened. While ransacking the flat, the burglar had seen the bank of pre-recorded videos but realised he couldn't carry them all. So he had telephoned his brother to see which ones he wanted. Not wanting to be implicated, the brother had immediately informed on the thief who was arrested 'red-eyed' watching another of the stolen tapes.

My Mummy Told Me

A cat burglar (so called for their stealth, not because the steal cats) broke into a Surbiton home early one morning. As he came through an upstairs window the burglar was shaken to hear a small voice saying, 'what do you want?"

Deciding not to run away the burglar replied, "where does your mummy keep her handbag?" Little four year old Darren was more than happy to help and showed him the way to a kitchen cupboard. Along side the handbag was a tin with gas and electricity money.

"My name's Darren Bailey. What's your name?" the little voice asked.
"John Roberts," the burglar replied, not wanting to frighten the little boy, "bye, see you later"

At breakfast the next day Darren's mother was asking everyone in the family if they had seen her handbag and money tin. Darren told her his little story about the activities that night. The police were called and Darren happily told his story again, complete with the burglars name. He was rewarded by a trip in a patrol car and easily spotted the burglar in an identity parade.

Trojan Horse

The concept of a Trojan horse has been copied by criminals all the way through history. One man from Swansea decided that he had a sure fire way of getting in to a bonded warehouse without being found. Once inside he would be able to take his pick of the warehouse's contents. He devised the plan of hiding inside a large crate. The package would then be delivered by courier to the warehouse getting him past security.

The scheme failed, however, when he miscalculated the delivery dates of the courier service. He had arranged for the 'parcel' to be picked up at 3pm on a Friday, specifying 'Next Day delivery'. Unfortunately he failed to realise that this particular courier did not deliver on Saturdays. By 5pm on the Saturday, stuck in the courier's depot, he had taken enough. Breaking out of his 'parcel' he called a mate to come and pick him up. This set off the courier's burglar alarms and he was arrested for breaking into the depot.

Who's Calling?

Having watched an episode of Crimewatch on TV a young criminal recognised himself as the wanted man in connection with an unpleasant mugging. Hoping to take attention away from himself he decided to phone up and give the name of an acquaintance thinking this would incriminate them and get him off the hook. He got through immediately and told the TV's phone answering crew which crime he had information about.

On being asked his name he gave it in full, with his address. "And who would you like to report?", he was asked, to which he gave his acquaintance's name. The police followed up the information but when the named man knew nothing about the incident they called on the 'informer'. He was duly arrested and charged. As the police said, "You can't get better than criminals informing on themselves!".

Lotta Bottle

B reaking in to people's houses can be thirsty work. That can be the only reason that a pair of house burglars helped themselves to a pint of milk after robbing a widow's bungalow one afternoon. On her return she was distraught to find her home broken in to.

After careful questioning in the kitchen by a female officer the old lady tutted that she had forgotten to wash the milk bottle out and went to tidy it up. A bit of quick thinking by the detective meant the bottle was rescued and tested for fingerprints. They matched a pair on file and the burglar was duly arrested. He had taken his gloves off to remove the milk bottle top.

Wrong Way

A 76 year-old lady stuck her tongue out at teenagers waving their arms at her car. "The youth of today have no respect," she muttered to herself.

She was later arrested and charged with dangerous driving having driven four miles the wrong way down a dual carriageway!

Channel Blunder

After many months of painstaking organisation a group of three robbers, two men and a woman accomplice, finally set off on their mission.

They had been monitoring the activities of a local ball-bearing firm having been made aware of the large sums of money that could be made selling these on the continent. One of the robbers had worked on the cross-sea ferries and was convinced he could sort out documentation for customs and get them through the port at Zeebrugge with no difficulty.

On the designated day the first man took an early ferry to Zeebrugge to await the arrival of the others with the truck the following day. His job was to make sure the lorry passed through customs successfully using his contacts.

The next day the second man and woman hijacked the company's biggest ball-bearing truck as it was due to make its weekly crossing from Hull to Zeebrugge. The truck driver was blindfolded, tied up and left in a nearby disused warehouse whilst his truck carried on its journey, this time driven by the robbers.

All went well and as the robbers relaxed on the overnight ferry they kept their fingers crossed that all would be well at the other end. Imagine their surprise then when the next morning the announcement came over the tannoy, "Good morning ladies and gentleman. We are about to dock at Rotterdam. Please make your way to your vehicles for disembarkation".

There was nothing the robbers could do, so they left as foot passengers. The lorry was left on board and caused a great deal of commotion. It was eventually removed and the driver traced and released. The ferry company could not understand how the lorry had got on the wrong ferry, but then mistakes do happen!

Call of Nature

A Glasgow mugger got himself in to deep trouble one hot summer's day. Being slight in stature he decided to dress up as a woman. His logic was that women would find it less threatening if he approached them. He could then distract their attention, nick their handbag and disappear in to the lunchtime crowds without being noticed. No one would suspect a woman carrying a bag.

His ruse worked for two days when he managed to steal four bags which were subsequently reported to police. He finally got his come-upance when the call of nature prevailed. Unable to go home, he decided to use a public loo.

Having queued for at least five minutes, as is standard in women's toilets, he was fit to burst. So much so that he rushed in and started to relieve himself without locking the door.

An equally desperate customer, seeing the open door burst in and saw what was obviously a man in ladies clothing. Her screams alerted the toilet attendant who managed to grab a passing policeman. The mugger was duly arrested and had to explain the contents of the handbag which contained ID that was not his.

No Way Out

Early lunch time shoppers in the genteel town of Harrogate, North Yorkshire, were shocked to see three armed men walking down the middle of one of their main shopping streets. The men were running and waving their guns and the distant wail of an alarm made the passers by soon realise this was not a theatrical hoax. A getaway car was waiting at the Cenotaph and it sped off as the police cars arrived.

The robbers, however, had not prepared their getaway and as they took the first left road available to them the police could not believe their luck. One cop car followed, while the other went on a parallel road. The reason? The robbers had shot up a long street which was in fact a dead-end. As they reached the wall and realised their mistake they all jumped out and ran off in different directions, two choosing to jump the wall. It was not long before they were caught. Jewellery from the raid was left in the getaway car.

Closed Doors

The owner of a shoe shop in Bristol called into his local building society to pick up a bag of cash to pay his workers. On the way out he noticed an unsavoury character, dressed mostly in black, watching his every move. As he walked around the corner towards his shop, the suspicious stranger, who turned out to be eager for money to buy drugs, started to follow.

After picking up the pace and turning two corners, the shoe shop owner realised something was wrong and started to run. The stranger also broke into a run. Turning another corner, the shop owner realised he'd come full circle and spotted the building society. He raced to the door and jumped inside. Then he waited for what seemed an eternity for the inside security door to flash green and let him inside - in this branch the second door will only open when the first is closed, giving the staff time to react in the case of a raid.

The stranger followed with his eye on the bag of money and didn't realise he was entering the lion's den. As the front door closed shut, the staff locked it and refused to open the inner door until the constabulary arrived.

Even On Holiday

They say that criminals are always on the look out for easy money. Here's the story of one convicted armed robber to show it's true. Michael Meyers had been recently released from jail after serving twenty months for an armed raid. His long suffering wife decided that they both needed a holiday to try and get back to a normal life again. So she booked for them to take a charter flight to Malaga for a week, staying at the apartment of a friend.

After a lovely fun packed week, without incident, the couple prepared to return home. Now, as you may be aware, to try to combat terrorism on planes, some companies require you to identify your luggage on the runway prior to boarding the plane. Any unclaimed luggage is removed.

Their flight was due to take-off when an announcement from the cabin crew was broadcast. "Good afternoon ladies and gentlemen. Welcome aboard our flight today from Malaga to Speke. We still have one item of luggage on the runway, a tan suitcase, which remains unclaimed. If this is yours please claim it now." Unable to stop himself Meyers claimed the suitcase and it was loaded.

On arrival at Speke airport on Merseyside the couple collected their luggage and moved through the green 'Nothing to declare' channel. They were stopped by an alert customs official who noticed that the tan suitcase was bulging whereas the other two were not.

On opening the case it was found to contain over 27lbs of pure grade Heroin. Meyers had a lot of explaining to do but was finally released uncharged.

Once But Not Twice

Amy Wilson, from Kettering, remembered the day her husband walked out on her. He'd just told her that he had lost his job and that they had no money left. His parting words were, "The bailiff will know doubt be round soon and I don't want to see him or you ever again". Amy was shocked but after twenty three years of marriage she was still very sad at the way things had ended. She and Tom had been childhood sweethearts, marrying very young.

Amy moved away from the home she had shared with Tom and went back to live with her mother in Inverness. But despite the separation they never actually filed for divorce.

Fifteen years later, whilst working as a council cleaner, she stopped to look at the newly married couple leaving the registry office. Imagine her surprise and then anger as she recognised her husband, Tom. Without thinking she ran over and tipped her bucket of water over him. The moment was captured on film by a local reporter and was front page news in the local paper the next day. Tom Wilson was charged with bigamy and as he was cautioned he was recorded to mutter, "I just knew I should have kept away from Scotland".

Burglar at Large

In the Summer of 1995 the police were called to a large residential home in Poole, Dorset after a ruby engagement ring belonging to one of the residents disappeared. The lady in question remembered leaving it on the basin window when she washed her hands and when she came back some few minutes later it was gone. A thorough search of the room by staff had not found it. Being rather senile the staff had assumed that the resident had mislaid it, but it could not be found.

Two days later police were again informed of the loss of some jewellery, this time a gold chain. The resident said she had taken it off when going to bed and left it on a dressing table by the window. In the morning it was gone. As she lived on the second floor it was unlikely that a passer by had pinched it.

Suspicion fell on a young male student who had started working at the home in his summer holidays. He protested his innocence and was vindicated when another theft was reported. Again it was a ring, but the young man was on his day off at the time.

Anxious to conclusively prove his innocence the young man decided to patrol the home's grounds to see if he could solve the mystery. His attention was caught early one morning by the antics of a group of magpies. To his amazement he saw one of the young magpies fly up to an open window and fly off with something shining it its beak. He watched the bird go to a nest. Returning to the home he passed on what he had seen and the police were told.

Using a 'platform-tuck', on hire from the council's lighting department, an RSPB representative was raised to the nesting site. Carefully he recovered a ruby ring, gold chain and diamond ring. Police declined to press charges but residents were asked to keep all jewellery away from opened windows.

Shoplifting Pain

Hiding items about your person has long been known as an effective way of lifting items from shops. Clothes can easily be worn without raising suspicion as you leave the store. Smaller items can be tucked away in pockets or bags. How then would you go about stealing a £250 cut glass vase from a china shop?

Maria Gainsborough had reckoned that her new large floppy velvet hat could be just the answer. With the hat in her hand she casually walked around the store. Out of view she picked up her chosen vase and put it in the hat. After a few minutes she put the hat on and pulled the side down firmly. Walking slightly oddly, keeping her back straight, she pushed the heavy glass doors and left the building.

At that instant a gust of wind swept round the corner throwing her hat into the air. As the vase crashed to the ground her arm was grabbed by a store detective who had been following the proceedings. The hat, now full of broken shards of glass was retrieved.

It's All Gone Dark

A sixteen year old teenager was keen to be seen wearing the best designer gear he could afford, or pinch. Deciding that the only essential item he lacked was some sunglasses he walked into a high street opticians. Noticing the top of the range Oakley's and Ray Ban's were in a locked glass case, he asked if he could try a pair on.

Having tried on various items and noticing that they cost over £100, he decided on the pair he would steal. He managed to distract the assistant serving him by asking her to adjust a pair so they fitted more tightly. He then took the pair that he wanted from the display. Putting them on and headed for the doors.

With a loud bang his exit was halted. He had walked straight into the glass double doors, his vision clouded by the very strong dark lenses. The assistant quickly returned to see her customer clutching a bleeding nose and bent sunglasses. The police were called but charges were not pressed as the youngster looked a sight for sore eyes.

Not Quite Superman

Clark Kent had to find somewhere to turn into Superman and telephone booths seemed to be quite useful for this purpose. When BT decided to change their company logo they also got rid of the traditional red telephone boxes replacing them with swish new glass kiosks.

Initially they were popular as they were clean and the phones usually worked. They did have one major problem, the occupants often got locked in and had to rely on a passer-by to open the door and let them out. This was not too much of a problem in busy town centres where people were queuing up to use the phone anyway. But in remote areas this was not always the case. Such a rogue kiosk existed in the seaside resort of Lynmouth, Devon.

Busy in the summer, this small seaside resort could be as quiet as a graveyard in winter. This did not deter a young car thief from checking out what was available in the bingo hall's car park one dark, wet, winters evening. Spotting a new reg Nissan in the car park he deftly opened the door and hot wired it.

About half a mile down the sea front he saw a telephone kiosk and pulled over to tell his contact the make and reg of the motor he had available to be disposed off. Having made his call he pushed the kiosk door - no luck. So he pulled. Still no luck. Frantically pushing and pulling the young thief became desperate.

As time moved on the glass misted up and the language inside deteriorated in a torrent of abuse. It was not helped by the approaching blue flashing light which crept up behind the white Nissan parked directly outside the telephone kiosk. Two police circled the car to make sure it was the one reported missing some half an hour earlier by a local bingo player. Noticing the steamed up telephone box they were reminded of recent SOS calls from the same place where occupants had become stuck.

As they opened the door the young man fell out and started to leg it up the sea front. Had he just said a polite 'thank you' and walked off the police may not have been suspicious. But his actions smacked of the guilty. He was arrested and charged with the theft, and his contact was also traced via the phone call. Just as well Superman did not have the same problems.

Caught in a tube

A pickpocket on the London Underground preyed on tourists. Knowing they were unfamiliar with our currency and surroundings he would relieve them of their wallets. Often he would watch to see how much they cashed at a bureau de change booth and then follow them around until a suitable moment arose.

This particular thief concentrated on foreign exchange booths near underground stations knowing that as they descended the escalators tourists often left wallets in the back of rucksacks and pockets. He would brush past on his way down the steps, remove the item, board a train and then leave at the next stop. This form of robbery is rife in cities such as London and there is very little the police can do except rely on the awareness of the general public.

One hot Saturday afternoon this particular thief was making his way down the escalator at Earl's Court when he saw a wallet protruding from the back pocket of a large tourist. As he lifted it he heard a growl of animal proportions, "Hey, that guy's got my wallet".

Without looking back the thief ran off down the steps and disappeared into the fast approaching crowd. Reaching the platform a train came in and he jumped on. The doors closed and the train began to move off just as the 'fat tourist' made it to the platform. He glared inside at his assailant.

On this day, however, London Underground came to the victim's aid. A blockage on the line a little further up caused the train to stop, the front half in the tunnel, the back half still at the platform. The doors opened and our thief had no time to get away as the American lurched into the carriage grabbing his enemy by the throat.

The wallet was returned amid much pleading for mercy, but our pick pocket was handed over to the police. He had, in fact, picked on a London Monarch American football star who was a lot fitter than he looked and who was certainly not afraid to have a go when duty called.

Slammer For You

Most robberies are spur of the moment opportunist ones. Someone sees a situation that could be to their gain and acts on impulse. An open door or a fallen wallet may be all that it takes. It was this sort of 'golden opportunity' which lay in wait for a local thief one warm autumn day. Walking through the leafy suburbs of his home in Sheffield the thief noticed three newspapers sticking out of a letterbox, and a pint of milk by the door. He called at the house and rang the doorbell.

As there was no answer he casually went around the back. All the signs of 'occupiers away' were there for him to see. Garden furniture was covered, children's toys were neatly stacked away and on peering through the windows he could see a newspaper with a headline that was at least four days old. He tried the back door which was securely locked, but a small window above the kitchen sink was loose and easily opened. He climbed in and had a good look around. Upstairs was some jewellery, some cash and a nice new portable TV.

As he descended the stairs he noticed some keys on a hook. One pair looked like car keys. He picked them up and made his way to the door at the bottom of the stairs which led to the garage. There to his delight there was a new looking Land Rover Discovery car. Our opportunist thief put his stolen goods in the back of the car using the hatchback door. He then hopped in and put the keys in the ignition. Problem.

The garage door was shut so he got out of the car and went too go back inside. As he reached the side door back into the house he noticed a little white button. On pushing this there was an almighty screeching noise which nearly had him running for his life. But, not to worry it was just the electronic garage door being activated.

With the loot in the boot, garage door open and car keys in hand our thief again hopped in and reversed out. Bang! The noise was deafening, our thief just didn't know what to do. He got out and walked round the back of the car. There was the garage door embedded in the roof of the Land Rover. A helpful passer-by saw the incident and came to the rescue. At this point our thief's nerves had taken enough and he ran off, but he didn't get far as the passer-by's dog was set upon him.

The police were called and the would-be thief arrested. It would seem that the garage door cord had been shut into the hatchback door. The cord was long enough to let the door go up automatically, but as the car reversed the cord pulled the garage door shut. On their return the occupiers were relieved that precious family jewellery had been saved and the car was repaired on their insurance.

Emperor's Clothes

A British family living in Gabon, West Africa were well aware of the risks of burglary. Their affluent lifestyle was a magnet for the wrong sorts in the poorer local population. Returning from a day out at a friend's homecoming barbecue the family did not think anything was wrong. They opened the front door and everything seemed OK. It was only when the husband went into his bedroom and saw the wardrobe door open that he thought something was wrong. Looking in to his wardrobe he noticed that all his shoes were missing. Not one pair but all.

He checked round the house trying not to alert his wife and two young children. There was no sign of forced entry and all the doors and windows were locked. After a discussion with his wife the local police were called. They visited the home of the maid who looked after the English family as she had a key to their house. Denying that she had had anything to do with the robbery the police left advising her to be more careful with her key. The next morning, as she waited to catch the bus to work at her English household she noticed the shoes on a fellow passenger. They were clean polished black leather which was unusual in this poor West African town. Recognising the man she said nothing but mentioned it to her employer on arriving at the house.

Her description of the shoes matched what the English man believed to be one of his pairs and the police were called again. Knowing who her fellow passenger was she was quick to tell the police his address to lift the blame from herself. On visiting his home they found all the stolen shoes neatly lined up under the bed. Under questioning he admitted to having 'borrowed' the key over the weekend and to having a bit of a penchant for Western leather shoes.

Examinated Win

One early summer's afternoon Gazza look-a-like James Bellows was studying in his small upstairs bedroom. With his 'A' levels fast approaching he was working extra hard on his Maths.

Looking out of the window he was surprised to see a man climbing a ladder that was propped up against the open window of their neighbour's bathroom. For a moment James thought it was the window cleaner but then the man noticed him watching and pulled a face with his tongue out!

James swiftly went downstairs and called the police who were waiting at the bottom of the ladder by the time the thief made his exit. James' neighbours were very grateful to him and were glad he was working so hard at his exams. When questioned the thief claimed he thought the real James was only a poster of the footballer stuck on a wall, and he pulled the face in imitation of the footballer's famous antics.

Pinned by a Pipe

If you want to break into a house by shinning up the drainpipe, pick a new house. That is the story John Goodman will be telling his fellow inmates after his attempted break in of a Victorian semi in Walthamstow.

Half way up the pipe, headed for a partially open side window, John heard a dull 'ping' followed by another. Seconds later he was flying through the air still holding on to the pipe which had torn away from the house.

He landed on his back in the middle of a flower bed in which several large rocks had been sprinkled as decoration. One of the rocks had broken his fall and ruptured his kidney. Needless to say his cries of pain showed the police the way to the scene of the crime.

Dateless

Off-licences are often the victims of crime. The odd bottle of whisky or wine will disappear nearly every night from shoplifters, but then there are the raiders. The main reason is the high price that the nicked items can fetch on the black market and the ease with which they can be disposed, and the usually large amounts of cash in the till.

It was with this in mind that three people plotted to raid an off-licence in the quaint market town of Banbury. Reckoning that at 2pm the shop would be pretty quiet they plotted the crime. One would charge in brandishing a fake shotgun whilst the other two would be waiting inside pretending to be customers. In the ensuing panic they would raid the till and lift some useful items. The fine details were planned along with the getaway and the group went their separate ways with synchronised watches.

The criminal whose job it was to burst in the shop with the gun was panicking as he walked along the high-street. He was about one minute late. With the gun stashed in a bag he stood outside the shop and pulled on his balaclava. Looking both ways he took out the gun and charged into the shop screaming like a Rambo look-alike. The lady behind the till looked terrified as he told her to lie on the floor.

Then all fell silent. No accomplices ran to the till. Looking around him all our hapless thief saw was an old man holding a bottle of Brandy with all the strength he could muster. Gathering his thoughts and realising that his colleagues were not about he quickly left the shop and legged it down the high-street to where he had parked the getaway car. Most of Banbury's shoppers saw this and it did not take too much police time to track him down. It would seem that he had turned up for the raid a day early.

I'd Like a Job Please

K nowing the high cost of photocopying, a female student in her final year at Reading University devised a plan. She needed to make at least one hundred copies of her CV to circulate to prospective employers and research institutions. When using the faculty photocopier students had to record the opening photocopy count from the machine before using it, and then note down the number after use. The difference was the number of copies they had had and they were charged cash accordingly. Staff could use the machine for university business by the same method, but instead of paying cash they put down a departmental account number.

Lindsey Jones knew the times that staff left the office and on Fridays it was always at 4.30 prompt in order to make an early start to the weekend. So she decided to break in to the university office at 7pm when she was sure the cleaners would have left. All went well as the office door was left unlocked. Confidential information and the computer were in a separate locked office.

She had let herself in, switched on the photocopier and waited for it to warm up. Inserting the three pages of her CV into the machine she pressed the counter for 100 copies and sat down. Fifteen minutes later all the copies were neatly stacked in the machine so she took them out and put them in her bag. Switching off the machine and light Lindsey departed certain that no one would know who'd 'stolen' the copies.

On the Monday morning when the secretary arrived to start work she followed her normal routine of switching on the photocopier and while it warmed up she made herself a coffee. The copy counter number was then noted down at the start of the log for the week. It was at this point she noted the discrepancy in the numbers from the last figure on Friday afternoon. Lifting the machine's lid she found Lindsey Jones' CV.

On being confronted about the item by her tutor, Lindsey confessed all. After a stern ticking off and confiscation of her copies by the department head she was let off with the advice that she did not follow a life of crime as she was clearly unsuited to it.

Goosed

Not all the criminals in this book are totally dumb. A lone robber who was targeting a rural area in Northumberland realised the threat posed by a pair of sheepdogs on a farm. So he invested in a couple of tasty steaks from the local butcher and drugged them with sleeping tablets.

The plan worked a treat and both dogs wolfed down the free meat. Within minutes they were both sound asleep and the path was open to our burglar. Unfortunately, being a townie type, he'd completely overlooked the geese who noisily surrounded him and held him at bay until the farmer arrived with his shotgun.

Father Christmas, He Got Stuck

D o you remember that childhood song? *Father Christmas, Father Christmas, He got Stuck, He got Stuck, Coming down the chimney, Coming down the chimney, What bad luck, What bad luck.* Well Windsor James from Birken-head either hadn't heard the song, or had forgotten it when he devised a scheme to come down the chimney of a nearby Manor House. If Father Christmas could do it - so could he.

He planned to burgle the house on Christmas Eve evening when the family was out at church. He spent several days surveying the house to see which chimneys were in use. Knowing the house to be old he estimated that the chimney would be quite wide. Being only 5' 9" and 10 stone he reckoned on being able to just slide down.

Watching the family leave he made his assault on the house. Not being totally stupid he did take a rope with him. After climbing on to the roof he tied the rope around a small chimney stack and lowered himself down the widest chimney. But his problems started straight away as the chimney was too narrow for him to bend his knees and climb down. So thinking of Father Christmas he just jumped in straight and let himself drop hoping his rope would stop him hitting the fireplace floor.

Alas he never got to find out as the chimney was narrower than he had imagined and he got totally stuck. Unable to free his legs and without the strength to pull himself up the rope he just lay there in a vertical position, stuck. Some hours later when the family returned they were bemused to hear muffled cries of help. Tracing the sound to a fireplace the teenage son of the house was amazed to see a pair of shoes when he shone a torch up the chimney.

The police and fire brigade were called and the thief eventually unceremoniously hauled out. Later the family did admit to wondering if Father Christmas was a true figure after all when they realised someone was stuck in their chimney.

Caught on Camera

K nowing that their raid on an electrical retailer was being filmed did not worry a particularly brazen set of criminals in the busy town of Newbury. They simply stole the incriminating video from the security system along with assorted loot from the shop - video recorders, TV's and satellite decoders. Everything was piled into a van and driven off.

When the burglary was discovered, along with the missing tape, the police realised they had little hope of catching the perpetrators. They struck lucky a few weeks later however. As part of an undercover operation, police officers were posing as the general public in a few notorious local public houses. When offered 'bargain' goods for sale the officers expressed an interest.

One was offered a 'brand new' VCR for less than £100. He duly paid cash for the item in the pub car park whilst other non-uniformed officers filmed the transaction. On taking the VCR to the police station to have it checked for being stolen a video cassette was found to be inside.

Curious, the officers played it back to find it wasn't the expected bootleg porno movie but the security video of the electrical shop robbery some weeks earlier. The grinning faces of the criminals were totally visible and recognisable and one was even the man that had sold the VCR to the police officer.

Rounding up the gang could not have been easier. Had it not been for their vanity in watching the video of their robbery, and of course their stupidity, they might never have been caught.

Too Neat

Pharmacies are often victims of drug users who can't afford to buy their requirements on the street. One such shop in Liverpool had taken precautions and locked all of their materials in a large safe following previous breakins. The local users were made aware of this arrangement and breakins to the pharmacy almost stopped overnight.

One user, however, went a step further upstream and broke into a doctors surgery to steal some prescription pads. Having written out his own prescription he then went into the pharmacy and handed over his slip.

The police were called and he was arrested. When asked why they had been alerted, one of the staff said, "The prescription was perfectly legible and written in block capitals. All of the doctors around here have totally indecipherable scrawls!"

Secret Switch

Police are still baffled as to how he managed it, but nevertheless it ranks as a dumb crime. A car was spotted swerving all over the road in Bristol. When the police cautioned the man it was obvious he had been drinking. The breath test proved positive and the driver opted to give a urine sample at the police station.

When the results came back from the laboratory it showed the driver hadn't been over the limit. In fact there wasn't a trace of alcohol to be found. However, it did show that he was more than five weeks pregnant.

Right on Time 1

A gang of youths were terrorising students in the University city of Oxford. The usual ploy would be to frog march their victims to a nearby cashpoint machine and use threats of violence to extort the money out of their accounts. Even though most students did as they were told, some still received a severe beating.

One student used his best weapon against the gang - his brain (actually a warthog probably has more intelligence than the entire band put together). When his cashpoint failed to render 'enough' loot the gang demanded more. The student replied that he could get some and that he'd bring it back at six o'clock. Amazingly one of the gang members kept the appointment and was greeted by three burly policemen.

Right on Time 2

A man walked up to the desk in a busy London station.

"I want to turn myself in for armed robbery," said the man.

"Look, can't you see I'm busy," replied the officer, used to dealing with cranks, "why don't you come back in a couple of hours."

He did, and was duly charged.

Barking Up the Wrong Tree

A man was arrested in a park for exposing himself to young girls. When questioned he claimed a jogger's dog had ripped all his clothes off in a vicious attack.

Endorsed

A handbag thief from Blackpool forged the true owner's signature on a cheque to pay for some clothes. Unfortunately she endorsed the back with her own name and real address.

Caught on Film

A middle aged French couple walked into a Kent police station to report the loss of their expensive SLR camera. But in the ladies handbag were a set of newly produced prints from a one-hour development shop and a second roll of film. The camera was found in their car.

Licence to be Dumb

The driver of a Vauxhaul Cavalier pulled into a petrol station, filled up the tank and drove off without paying. The owners had taken precautions against being spotted by squirting shaving foam over the licence plates.

Unfortunately the speed at which they tried to escape the scene caused the foam to be blown away revealing the registration to the security cameras monitoring the situation.

Wrong Plug

An opportunist thief entered an electrical shop in Clapham, unplugged a mini hifi centre without the staff seeing what he was doing. With his car parked outside with the engine running, his plan was to grab the hifi and run out of the shop before anyone could react.

But as he lurched for the door the hifi was pulled out of his hands and fell to the ground. He'd unplugged the wrong one!

Hansel & Gretel

Police didn't have much problem tracing a shop looter following a small scale riot in a south coast town. They simply followed the trail of blood to his door. When the thief opened the door he tried to explain away his bandaged wrist as a "slip with a kitchen knife" until the police showed him the red spots marking his movements.

Over the Pond

New York lottery officials reported a lady who had tampered with her lottery ticket to claim a prize of $20 which she didn't deserve. The ticket she'd invalidated would have won her $5,000

Bungled Bribe

A Birmingham man was pulled over for speeding in his ageing Fiat and then tried to bribe the officer with a carton of cigarettes. As he finished writing the speeding ticket and prepared to book him for attempted bribery, the officer noticed the carton was one of around twenty on the back seat. Back at the station the man confessed to having just raided a local off-licence.

Grounds for Divorce

A Welsh woman refused to pay a parking fine by insisting her husband had been driving the car at the time. It turned out she wasn't married.

The Gun Shop

Not a great deal needs to be said about the Leeds man who walked into a gun shop one day, locked into Rob-The-Place mode, brandishing – wait for it – a replica gun!

The shopkeeper was not impressed and immediately set about showing the bandit, in extreme close-up, what a real firearm looked like. The robbery was unsuccessful. Very.

Caught With Copies

Forging bank notes is a crime that has been on the go ever since bank notes existed. Some are works of art detectable only by modern machines, others look less realistic than Monopoly money.

One retired Civil servant in Maidenhead had been circulating forged notes for years without being detected. Recently, however, more notes had been found by local stores on presenting them to their bank. No one likes to lose money, least of all shopkeepers, and so the forgeries had been notified to police. No action had been taken but the matter was in hand.

If it had not been for an alert clerk at the council offices the forger may have remained at large. He was discovered when he tried to pay a small parking fine with a forged £20 note.

The cash clerk spotted the forgery and along with council regulations called the police straight away. The main police station being only a block away an officer was at the council cash office within minutes.

The man protested his innocence but the arresting officer smelt a rat when the man's wallet contained three other similar forgeries. On searching his small flat a substantial amount of forgery equipment was found.

As the officer explained, "It's one thing to use forged notes to pay for groceries, but it's the height of cheek to pay a fine with them".

Key Witness

In the early '90s Ram Raids became quite common. Shops, and sometimes even whole streets erected stone pillars to stop the relentless onslaught of cars, vans and trucks reversing into store fronts. The goods would then be piled into the van for the one or two minutes it took the police to be alerted, and then the vehicle would drive off leaving a smashed shop, often with alarms blaring.

One sports shop in Manchester was fed up to the back teeth with being regularly ram raided. All measures from concrete pillars to metal cage doors seemed to fail under the relentless attacks from various raids.

One particular wet autumn night the shop alarms went off again and the owner was alerted by police. On arriving at his shop in the early hours expecting to see the usual scene of decimation, the shop owner was amazed to see a seven-ton truck wedged in his shop front. The driver and accomplices were being led away to a waiting police van.

"What happened," the man asked, "did it get stuck in the shop front?"

"No," the officer replied, "they dropped the keys and couldn't find them!".

Stolen Twice

As any owner will know, a car can look like it has been round the world twice but can also be as reliable and cheap to run as a loyal dog. One such 'P' reg Ford Escort was owned by Julian Manning in London.

His blue car was covered in bumps, scratches and dents, the heater did not work and he had recently lost the ignition key. That did not worry its owner as this car did well on petrol and always started with the help of a screwdriver. People gave it a wide berth at roundabouts and, anyway, who would want to steal such a wreck.

But on leaving work one evening Manning walked to where he always parked his car. In its place was a new Frontera 4x4. Manning could not believe it. Standing on the pavement he tried to remember where he had left the car, knowing full well he had left it there, where it no longer was.

After several minutes he returned to work and called the police. Giving full details, still incredulous that anyone would nick his motor, he was advised that the police would contact him when the car was found. The car was insured third party for £150.

Later that evening Mr Manning was delighted to be called by the police who said that the car had been spotted parked outside a large block of flats in Tower Hamlets. As the car did not have any licence plates on it the police asked Mr Manning to accompany them to the car and confirm it was his. On arrival the car was not where it should have been.

The officer driving the patrol car was as shocked as Julian had been some hours earlier when it had first been stolen. "Well it was here twenty minutes ago," the officer told him, "I saw it myself." At that moment a youth appeared from the broken door of the block's main stairwell. He hesitated at the spot where the car should have been and then looked around. Seeing the police car he pulled up his collar and walked off.

Swiftly the two uniformed officers in the car pursued him and brought him back to the car. After a few minutes questioning he admitted stealing the car from outside Julian's workplace. As a mechanic he had planned to take it to his lock-up garage and strip it down for parts.

It would seem that in the hour that he had left it outside his flat it had been nicked again. The man was arrested and Mr Manning taken home. His car was never found. Police think it was most liked used for joy riding and then left to burn on disused land somewhere. An ignominious end to a well loved friend really.

The Car Thief

It's a sad fact that too many people leave their car keys in the ignition and the car doors open when filling up at petrol stations, especially on the newer models where the key is not needed to unlock the petrol cap first. Thieves hide behind unused pumps and simply run over and steal the car whilst the owner is paying the cashier in the shop. However, it is undoubtedly a good idea to let the owner actually fill up first.

One such opportunist thief, being far too eager for his own good, happened to steal a car at a Birmingham petrol station, whilst the hapless owner was inside the shop asking the equally hapless cashier (they always are) what kind of fuel the vehicle actually ran on.

Running entirely on fumes, the car suddenly raced out of the forecourt and promptly stopped dead some thirty yards down the way, where the confused thief jumped out and ran off.

Chased by both the owner and the irate cashier, the thief ran across the main road and was hit by a Number Six bus. He no doubt spent the next three years in prison ruing his stupidity and the fact that his footballing days were over.

What? My Car?

Fed up with his clapped out old rusting 'C'-reg Volkswagen a man from Norwich decided to report it stolen. Calling in to his local police station he explained how the car had been stolen from outside his work place. Details were taken and the man left with the duty sergeant telling him he would be contacted when it turned up.

The man left and returned home. His car, reported stolen, was noticed by a passing patrol car parked in the car park of the police station.

Officers called at the man's house and after detailed questioning managed to get him to admit it was all a scam. He had driven it to the police station to report it missing and then left it in their car park.

Going Solo

A man who obviously distrusted getaway drivers (or was simply too greedy to share the loot) parked up outside a London Post Office one sunny day in August '94, and left the motor ticking over whilst he dashed inside to rob the place.

Inside, he shouted at the surprised pensioners and various other customers to hit the deck. Then, being a rather noisy sort, proceeded to yell at a cashier to fill a Tesco carrier bag with money, training a sawn-off shotgun at her face as a gentle persuader. In an incredibly brave move, she stuffed bag after bag of cash into the carrier, together with a few handfuls of fake notes on hand specifically for occasions such as this.

Once outside, the robber found that his geta-way vehicle was gone – stolen! He was left clutching a bag full of ten pence coins (to a total value of £55) and a whole load of dud notes (to a total value of zilch).

As if things weren't bad enough, when he started to run the flimsy carrier bag split open and what little loot he had ended up in the road. Finally, as if further proof were needed that his MENSA application should've gone straight in the bin, he decided to make his geta-way by bus and was caught trying to dodge the fare! What a guy! He got six years.

Brought to Book

Anyone who has owned a bicycle will know the hassle involved in securing it. Yet it only takes a second for a casual passer-by to hop on your bike and make off with it. Reporting a bike as being stolen may help an insurance claim, but it is unlikely to ensure a prompt return. So it is worth taking just a few seconds to secure your bike, wherever you are.

Marcia Hinds will always lock her bike up know matter where she is following her recent experience. It all started on a warm summer's day in June. Needing to return a library book, Marcia just rested her bike against the wall before going in to the library.

Less than two minutes later she was back out again and saw that her bike had gone. Almost at the same time she heard a terrible crash and looked across the road to see a bike tangled up on the bumper of a bus. The rider was no where to be seen but a woman's scream alerted on-lookers to the fact that he was probably under the bus.

An ambulance took the injured man away and the police asked around for witnesses. Marcia told them that it was her bike and that she had just noticed it stolen from the library. It would seem that the young thief had snatched the bike and in his haste to be off he had ridden it straight in front of the oncoming bus.

Keep on Trying

A small rural village often has the 'village idiot'. This person is usually harmless, just a bit dim. In one such farming community in Cleveland, there is a village idiot who just can't stop himself pinching things that are not his. His penchant is for 'walk-in' burglaries. The name comes from the fact that the victim leaves a door or window open and the criminal just 'walks-in' grabbing what they can before leaving.

Bearing in mind that he would probably be recognised anyway in this close knit area, an unfortunate facial deformity in the form of a massive mole on his nose means he is instantly recognisable by neighbours and passers by after he has carried out the crime. The police just call round to his home and recover the goods then return them to their rightful owners.